We Shake in a Quake

Hannah Gelman Givon
Illustrations by David Uttal

TRICYCLE PRESS
Berkeley, California

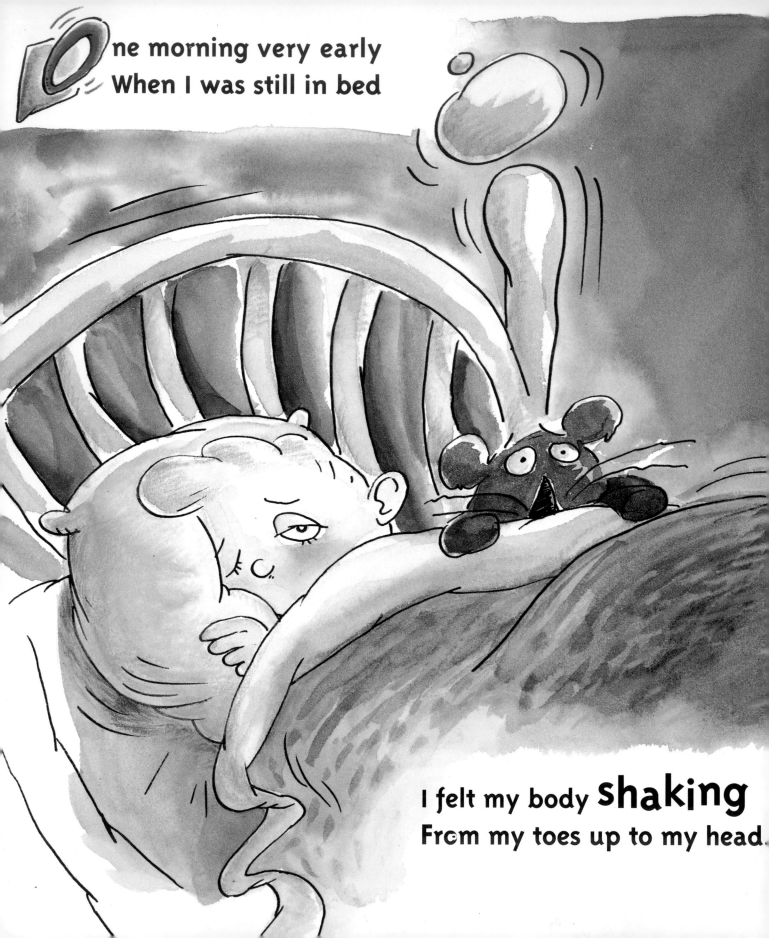

One morning very early
When I was still in bed

I felt my body **shaking**
From my toes up to my head.

I didn't dare
to make a move.
What was
I to do?
Then suddenly
I noticed
That my
bed was
shaking, too!

In fact, the *house* was shaking!
I wondered how it could.

Then I remembered—EARTHQUAKE!
And then I understood.

quickly jumped down to the floor—
queezed underneath my bed
Away from windows that could break,
With my hands behind my head.

I called out to
my Daddy,
To Grandpa,
and to Mom.
I wanted them
to come
RIGHT NOW!
But I tried to
stay real calm.

It isn't easy to be cool
In the middle of a quake.
You can't help feeling kind of scared
When you shake and shake—and **shake.**

I waited there beside my bed
Until the final shake,
And then I looked around my room—
"**WOW!** What a monster quake!"

Then at last I heard some steps
And got up from the rug.
Mom and Daddy rushed to me
With kisses and a hug.

Then Grandpa and my sister came,
We all said we were scared.
We all agreed that scary feelings
Needed to be shared.

We walked together through the house—
The mess was everywhere.
But Grandpa winked and smiled at me,
"These things we can repair."

Three flower pots had broken
And sprayed the floor with dirt.
But Dad said, "Not important.
None of *us* were hurt."

A vase had tipped right over,
The daisies looked so wilted.

And on the wall right down the hall
Our pictures all were tilted!

So many things had left their place—
We cleaned our house all day,
And talked and talked about the quake
(We had a lot to say).

Said Mom, "We must be ready
As a quake could come again."
Said Dad, "You're right, let's make a plan.
Here's paper and a pen."

Then Sis and I—we asked our mom
What kids like us could do
To help the grown-ups to prepare
(It was *our* earthquake, too).

So the next day we went shopping,
Sis and Mom and me.
We bought dried fruits,
and cans of food,
And powdered milk, and tea.

Three water jugs for each of us
(For safety we chose plastic),

Some handi-wipes,
some snacks for Max—
Mom said we were **fantastic!**

Some flashlights and a radio
That work by battery,
'Cause sometimes during big, bad quakes
There's no electricity.

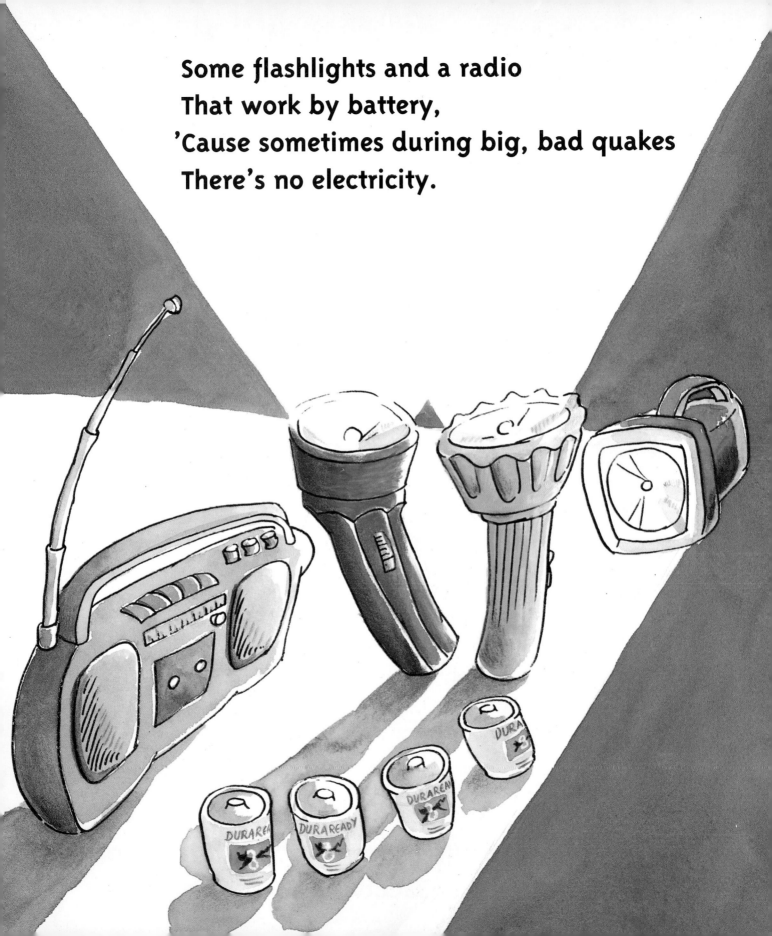

We had to find a safe, snug place
To store our new supplies.
We chose the closet in the hall.
Do *you* think we were wise?

We packed some blankets, first aid kit
And Mommy's warmest shawl,
The water, food, and radio—
In fact, we packed it all!

I stashed my flashlight and my boots
Right underneath my bed.
They'll help to keep me safe from harm
From my toes up to my head.

Later Grandpa sat us down
To check through our big list.
"I think we've got it all," he said.
"There's nothing that we've missed!"

The morning I went back to school
My friends had lots to say.
We talked about the earthquake
And how we felt that day.

The whole school practiced earthquake drills
As fast as we were able.

We learned to **"drop and cover"**
And to crouch beneath a table.

Our teacher showed us some good books
To teach us more on quakes.
We looked at pictures of the Earth
And learned what makes the **shakes.**

The Earth is round and solid,

The top of it is rock.

The rock's divided
into "plates"
Which move—
and sometimes knock.

But now and then these giant plates
May give a sudden **shove**
Which bumps and shakes and bounces
Whatever is above.

So bridges, roads, and houses shake,
And even trees can shiver.
The water sloshes in your tub
And also in the river.

I listened to my teacher,
Then on my drawing pad
I drew some **MONSTER** pictures
'Cause I was feeling mad!

I drew some **BOOs** and **BAHs** and **BOOMs**
And lots of shaky dashes.
I built some buildings with my blocks
And knocked them down in crashes!

I like *that* kind of earthquake
Because it's just pretend.
When I get tired of shaking
I simply make it end!

I'm kind of glad it's over—
It wasn't any fun.

But we'll be ready for the shake
When we have another one.

Earthquake Words to Know

aftershock: A less-severe quake that follows the stronger main earthquake.

core: The center of the Earth.

crust: The rocky outer layer of the Earth, where people, plants, and animals live. The crust floats on the mantle.

earthquake: A shaking of the ground caused by the sudden breaking and shifting of the Earth's rocky crust. The crust breaks because of stress put on it by the moving plates. When the crust breaks, a lot of energy is released which makes the ground vibrate, or shake. Volcanic eruptions can also set off a quake.

epicenter: The point on the ground that is right above the point inside the Earth where a quake starts.

fault: A crack in the Earth's crust where an earthquake happens.

mantle: A thick, very hot layer between the Earth's core and its crust, mostly made of melted rock.

plates: Very large pieces of the Earth's crust. There are about twelve plates that cover the Earth. They are always moving and trying to pass each other, which puts stress on the rocky crust.

Richter scale: A scale of numbers that describes the energy released by an earthquake, or its strength. A quake that measures six on the Richter scale is ten times stronger than one that measures five. The strength of a quake depends on how much energy was released.

seismograph: A machine that measures and records earthquake shakes.

tremor: A small earthquake.

tsunami: A giant ocean wave caused by an underwater earthquake or volcano.

Dear Children and Family,

Nobody likes earthquakes, but there are some things that you can do to feel safer. Contact your local Earthquake Safety or Disaster Preparedness Center for information (check under the city government listings in your phone book). Read books about earthquakes to increase your knowledge and decrease your fear. Make sure your family plans for where, how, and when to meet in different scenarios (at home, at work, at school, at the park, etc.) during a disaster. Agree on a long-distance telephone contact with whom the whole family can check in. Know where the gas and water shut-off valves are in your home. Secure heavy furniture and pictures to walls. Check your chimney, roof, walls, and foundation for stability.

REMEMBER, DURING AN EARTHQUAKE...

- Stay calm
- Don't jump out of bed barefoot
- Get under a table, desk, or bed, or stand in a doorway. Keep away from windows, or heavy, unsecured furniture and mirrors. Protect your head!

AFTER AN EARTHQUAKE:

- Check for injuries and safety (fires, etc.)
- Turn on your portable radio
- Be prepared for aftershocks
- Use telephones for emergencies only
- Know that children may have difficulty sleeping or separating from parents
- Hug each other!

This list can help you prepare your home for an earthquake:

- ❏ Flashlights with extra batteries
- ❏ Transistor radio with extra batteries
- ❏ A first aid kit with handbook and any necessary medication (for one week)
- ❏ Pipe and crescent wrenches for shutting off gas and water
- ❏ Fire extinguisher
- ❏ Three gallons of water in plastic containers for each member of the household
- ❏ Canned food (for one week) for your family and pets
- ❏ A manual can opener
- ❏ A family plan of action and a neighborhood plan
- ❏ Sturdy footwear, blankets, a change of clothes, and work gloves
- ❏ Emergency telephone numbers
- ❏ Money
- ❏ A leash for your pet

To my loving inspirations,
Eve and Ilana and their families.
To my creative book partner, David.
Thank you always to Lucky Roberts.
—H.G.G.

For Hannah and Nicole with gratitude.
And for Nancy: Love and support
will guide us over all this shaky ground.
—D.U.

Library of Congress Cataloging-in-Publication Data
Givon, Hannah Gelman.
    We shake in a quake / Hannah Gelman Givon; illustrated by David Uttal.
        p. cm.
    Summary: Rhyming text captures a boy's experience during and after
an earthquake and discusses ways to prepare for such a disaster.
    ISBN: 1-883672-25-2 Casebound / ISBN: 1-58246-022-1 Paperback
    1. Earthquakes—Juvenile literature. 2. Earthquakes—Safety measures—
Juvenile literature. [1. Earthquakes.] I. Uttal, David, ill. II. Title
QE521.3.G58 1996
551.2'2'0289—dc20

                                    96-2227
                                    CIP
                                    AC

First Tricycle Press printing, 1996
First paperback printing, 1999
Printed in Singapore

2 3 4 5 6 7 8 — 03 02 01